MICHELE BASSO

GUIDE
to the
VATICAN NECROPOLIS

FABBRICA DI S. PIETRO IN VATICANO

PREFACE

It is often said that, to get a real idea of what ancient Rome was like in the period of the Empire's greatest expansion, one should see Ostia, not Pompei or Herculanum.

Speaking of Rome, I am not referring to the monumental city of imperial palaces, nor of splendid temples, but to the city where daily life pulsated in the streets teeming with people from every part of the world – a hive of humanity with its public places, stores, exotic cults, etc.

To have an idea of the ancient Roman cities of the dead, do not go to the great imperial mausoleums: they are an exception to the norm; neither should you go to the rows of tombs which flank the Appian Way. You should rather go to the necropolis discovered beneath St. Peter's Basilica in 1939.

Here we see how tombs were crowded on the outskirts of the city; they line the narrow streets of the necropolis like little houses, complete with their neatly-built brick facades, with doors and windows and the names of the deceased on the epigraphs. If you stoop down to look inside, you can see beautiful stucco and fresco decorations on the walls, mosaics on the floor, and even some sarcophagi that are exquisite works of art.

There are better examples of this type of second-century tombs those of via Latina, those incorporated into the catacombs of S. Sebastiano, or the "Temple of Redicolo" in the Caffarella valley. These tombs, however, are often isolated and distant from one another; furthermore, they lack furnishings and sarcophagi: in times past they were looted as soon as they were discovered; all that was left was the simple yet precious skeleton.

At St. Peter's, however, we are faced with a situation similar to that of Pompei or Herculanum; there the eruption of Vesuvius suddenly sealed the city beneath a layer of stones and ash; here, however, Constantine's architects were ordered to build quickly a huge Basilica over the burial place of the Prince of the Apostles and so they covered the Vatican cemetery with earth.

Here we can also see the "memoria" of Peter's tomb: a red wall and the remains of the "Trophy of Gaius"; a modest amount, to be sure, in comparison to the glory of the altar of the *Confessio* and Michelangelo's dome rising above it. For this very reason, though, it is more suggestive and richer in inspiration as it reminds us of the faith with which Christians throughout the centuries have venerated this sacred shrine.

With this guidebook Mons. Basso has successfully presented a clear and simple informative synthesis of the archaeological complex located beneath St. Peter's. It will be of great help to all who come to visit the Vatican Necropolis, giving them an idea of life as it was viewed in the ancient Roman "city of the dead".

Carlo Pietrangeli
*Director General of
the Pontifical
Monuments, Museums
and Galleries*

Longitudinal cross-section (west-east)
I - BASILICA. II - VATICAN GROTTOES. III - PRE-CONSTANTINIAN BASILICA.

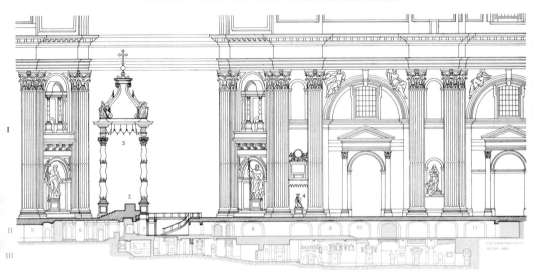

I - BASILICA - 1) St. Peter's tomb - 2) Papal altar of Clement VIII - 3) Bernini's canopy - 4) Bronze statue of St. Peter.

II - VATICAN GROTTOES - 5) Tomb of Pius XII - 6) Clementine Chapel - 7) "Confessio Sancti Petri" - 8) Tomb of John XXIII - 9) Tomb of John Paul I - 10) Tomb of Paul VI - 11) Tomb of Boniface VIII.

III - MAUSOLEUMS OF THE PRE-CONSTANTINIAN NECROPOLIS - A) "Popilius Heracla". E) "Aelius Tirannus". F) "M. Caetennius Antigonus". H) "C. Valerius Herma". O) "T. Matuccius Pallas". *) "Clivus" and the "Red Wall".

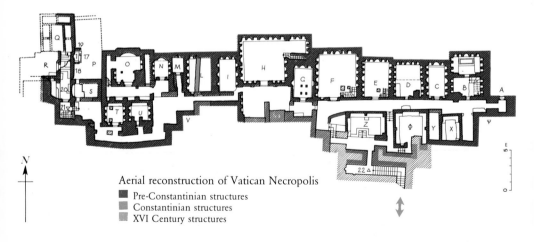

Aerial reconstruction of Vatican Necropolis
■ Pre-Constantinian structures
■ Constantinian structures
■ XVI Century structures

6

VATICAN NECROPOLIS "AD CIRCUM"

The whole area on the west bank of the Tiber River, extending from the Milvian Bridge to the Janiculum, was referred to in ancient times as the "Vatican", "Vatican Fields", or "Vatican Hills".

The hilly part of this area consisted of banks of clay and sand which were exploited for the manufacture of bricks, tiles, and pottery. The valley, on the other hand, was full of snake-infested marshes. The land was planted with vineyards which produced a wine of inferior quality.

The consular roads — *Aurelia, Trionfale* and *Cornelia* — ran from the Neronian bridge across this fourteenth district of the city of Rome. In the Vatican area the remains of notable monuments have been discovered, such as the "hippodrome" called Gaianum, a Phrygianum, a temple dedicated to the goddess Cybele, and one of the two "Naumachie", places for mock naval battles.

The Circus of Caligula and Nero

In the area between the present Vatican Hill and the Janiculum, Agrippa Maior, mother of Caligula, built large gardens called the "Horti Neroniani"; here Caligula began construction of the famous circus which, when completed by Nero, was called the "circus of Caligula and Nero".

Caligula also erected a large Egyptian obelisk in the circus, about ten meters below the present ground level. This obelisk remained there until 1586 when Pope Sixtus V had it transferred to St. Peter's Square by the architect Domenico Fontana; he marked the original site with a stone inscribed "SITO DELL'OBE-LISCO VATICANO FINO ALL'ANNO MDLXXXVI" — the site of the Vatican obelisk until 1586.

The "titulus" found over the door of Mausoleum A, which is still in place, bears the inscription of a certain "Popilius Heracla", who expressed the wish to be buried "IN VATIC. AD CIRCUM", that is, in the Vatican by the Circus.

As in many suburban areas, in fact, the Vatican was also crowded with tombs. The necropolis beneath St. Peter's Basilica is a famous example, as is seen by the variety and state of preservation of the monuments that have been excavated there.

Martyrdom and burial of Peter

The Apostle Peter, leader of the Christian community of Rome, martyred in the Circus of Caligula and Nero during the persecutions of 64-67 A.D., was buried in a nearby tomb on the slopes of the Vatican Hills, in accordance with Roman funeral law. The site of his tomb has actually been found there, and is proved to have been the object of special veneration throughout the centuries.

As early as 150 A.D., within the shelter of a red-plastered wall, a small funeral monument, referred to as the "Trophy of Gaius", was erected there; among other things, one of the small marble columns which adorned it can still be seen on the site.

The Basilica of Constantine

The Vatican Necropolis, begun and developed as a pagan burial place, was in use until the beginning of the fourth century; the Emperor Constantine, who had granted freedom to the

Christian cult with the Edict of Milan in 313, decided to build a basilica-martirium over the tomb of St. Peter. He stipulated that the level of the pavement should be even with the level of the Trophy of Gaius.

Constantine's architects therefore levelled the hill, cutting off any parts of the tombs that would protrude above the new floor level. They built massive retaining walls and filled the whole area with surplus earth, constructing a huge platform on which the Constantinian basilica would be built.

The Emperor Constantine enclosed the venerated tomb in a marble monument in the centre of the apse of the Basilica; this monument was called the "Memoria Costantiniana".

The Paleo-Christian basilica, consisting of five naves and an atrium surrounded by a portico, was partially destroyed in 1502. In 1506 Pope Julius II ordered the construction of a new Basilica in Renaissance style; his desire was to honour the tomb of the apostle which, throughout the centuries had become the object and centre of faith and art.

Archaeological investigation of the Vatican
Necropolis (1939-1951)

In 1939 Pope Pius XII sponsored archaeological excavations beneath the pavement of the Vatican Grottoes, the tombs of the Popes. This research produced the successful discovery of the tomb of St. Peter, the prince of the Apostles. This tomb has been identified with scientific precision; it is located directly beneath the papal altar, in direct line with Bernini's canopy and the dome.

The direction of the excavations was entrusted to His Excellency Msgr. Ludovico Kaas, financial secretary of the Commission for the Maintenance of St. Peter's; he was assisted by technicians of that same department and by the engineers Galeazzi and Nicolosi, along with Professors Josi, Apolloni-Ghetti, and the Jesuits Kirschbaum and Ferrua. Excavations were completed in 1951. There was unanimous agreement regarding the archaelogical and historical research; the official report on the discoveries appears in the two volumes entitled: ESPLORAZIONI SOTTO LA CONFESSIONE DI SAN PIETRO IN VATICANO (Explorations Beneath the Confessio of St. Peter's in the Vatican).

10

Vatican Necropolis
(Passageway)

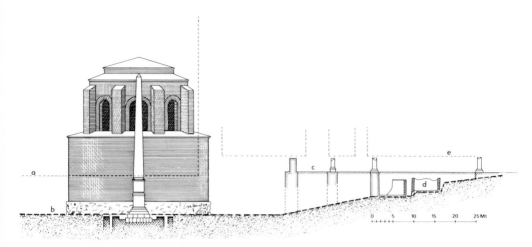

Section of the area of the obelisk and the Necropolis of the Vatican Grottoes: *a* present ground level, *b* ground level of the circus, *c* Constantinian basilica, *d* necropolis, *e* present Basilica (G. Ioppolo)

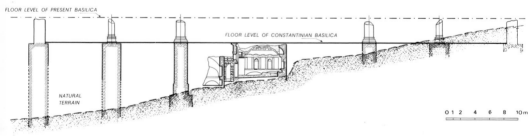

Cross section (south → north) beneath the floor level of the Constantinian Basilica in the area of Mausoleum "*F*", "Tomb of (M.) Caetennius Antigonus"

12

MAUSOLEUMS

MAUSOLEUM "Z"
"The Egyptian tomb"

MAUSOLEUM "Z" – "The Egyptian tomb"

This tomb is called "the Egyptian tomb" because of the picture of Horus, an Egyptian god of the dead, which is painted in the centre of the north wall of the tomb.

The roof of the mausoleum is missing because it protruded above the floor level of the Constantinian Basilica; the facade was also demolished by Constantine to erect one of the three retaining walls needed to support the fourth century Basilica. The façade was directly in line with the foundation wall of the Basilica, beneath the columns which separated the central nave from the first nave to the south.

Six sarcophagi and four *arcosolia* (a niche for interment surmounted by an arch) were found in the tomb of reddish plaster. There is also evidence of probable cremations.

The left sarcophagus on the north wall has a mythological scene in which we see Dionysius in a chariot driven by a centaur; he is accompanied by fauns, bacchants and corybants; Arianna is asleep in the depths of a forest. The front of the cover, depicting an aerial dance of maenads, seems to crown the bacchanal scene of the sarcophagus.

Mausoleum "Z" - "The Egyptian Tomb"
(Bacchanal sarcophagus)

16

Mausoleum "Z" - "The Egyptian Tomb"
(Detail of the Bacchanal sarcophagus)

MAUSOLEUM "Φ" - "Tomb of the Marci"

MAUSOLEUM " Φ " – "Tomb of the Marci"

The title of the tomb denotes the name of the owners of the one large sarcophagus found there; according to the inscription, it was placed in the Vatican Necropolis by the owners while they were still alive: "Q. Marcius Hermes Sibi et Marciae Thrasonidi dignissimae coniugi vivis posuit" ("Marcius Hermes himself and Marcia Thrasonidi, his most devoted wife, still living, put this here") is engraved on the front of the cover, where a bas-relief depicts two dead persons surrounded by funerary genii.

The sarcophagus, sculptured with excellent grace, is one of the best discovered in the Vatican necropolis. It depicts in full relief from left to right: a maenad, Dionysius with a young satyr and a faun at his feet; a satyr with the god Bacchus as a child.

On the walls there are several subjects from Greek mythology; on the west wall, to the left of the entrance, a painting of a peacock is still visible. On the south wall are two niches for cineraria. On the outside wall, to the left of the entrance, are the remains of a small Roman mosaic.

Mausoleum "Φ" - "Tomb of the Marci"
(Front of the Sarcophagus)

Mausoleum " Φ " - "Tomb of the Marci"
(North wall)

Mausoleum " Φ " - "Tomb of the Marci"
(West wall)

Mausoleum " Φ " - "Tomb of the Marci"
(East wall)

22

Mausoleum " Φ " - "Tomb of the Marci"
(Fragment of a wall mosaic)

MAUSOLEUM "A" - "Tomb of Popilius Heracla"

MAUSOLEUM "A" – "Tomb of Popilius Heracla"

This tomb is unexplored to date, and still contains the land-fill. It is one of the most important tombs because of the "titulus" which gives us the name of the owner and his request; he asked his heirs to have a tomb constructed near that of Ulpius Narcissus in the Vatican near the circus.

MAUSOLEUM "B" - "Tomb of Fannia Redempta"

MAUSOLEUM "B" – "Tomb of Fannia Redempta"

Tomb B, or the "Tomb of Fannia Redempta" is subdivided into two parts, denoted as B and B^1, the entrance and main part respectively; thus we see that typical elements of a house of the living can also be found in the "house of the dead".

On the walls of the first room are the rows of niches used for holding the cineraria, urns or vases to contain the ashes after cremation; these are indicative of a pagan burial.

In the second room, besides other cineraria, there are some interments in *arcosolia*. The walls are all frescoed with flower and animal designs.

The vault has a fresco with the allegory of the "Sun Chariot", surrounded by molded figures of the seasons.

This very ancient tomb shows some divergences; the vault is still original, but the walls have been modified, first to accommodate new burials and later again at the time of the work on the Constantinian basilica.

MAUSOLEUM "C" – "Tomb of (L.) Tullius Zethus"

MAUSOLEUM "C" – "Tomb of (L.) Tullius Zethus"

The *titulus* above the entrance indicates the owner, (L.) Tullius Zethus and his family.

This tomb is one of the most ornate, with its mosaic wall and floor decorations, partly polychrome and partly black and white.

There are niches for cineraria and two *arcosolia*. In the north wall two marble urns have been added at a later period; these have typically Christian design elements, such as the laurel wreath and palm.

Mausoleum "C" – "Tomb of (L.) Tullius Zethus"
(Interior)

Mausoleum "C" – "Tomb of (L.) Tullius Zethus"
Mosaic floor with partridges and ivy-leaf design.

MAUSOLEUM "D" – "Opus reticulatum Tomb"

MAUSOLEUM "D" – "Opus reticulatum Tomb"

The name of this tomb derives from the structure of its walls, made of small blocks of pumice, in a pattern known as "opus reticulatum".

The funeral room is still covered by the ceiling; on its walls there are many niches with cineraria.

A wall built during the Constantinian era closed the entrance of the tomb; a large terracota pipe has been placed in it, either to facilitate the flow of water, or as a probable drain.

MAUSOLEUM "E" – "Tomb of (T.) Aelius Tyrannus"

MAUSOLEUM "E" – "Tomb of (T.) Aelius Tyrannus"

The titulus of this tomb is no longer in place, although the elegant multicolored terracotta frame remains; the name of the tomb is derived from an inscription on a stone found inside the *arcosolium* on the left-hand wall. The owner is (T.) Aelius Tyrannus, a freedman who came to take up a public office in the administration of the Roman province of the Belgica region of Gaul.

The most interesting details in this tomb are the two alabaster cineraria placed inside equally-decorated niches. Among the stucco figures and pictures decorating the walls, one should take note of two peacocks beside a basket of flowers, birds in flight and funerary genii.

There are arcosolia and niches for cinerary urns in the walls; there are also the remains of the mosaic pavement in small pieces of black and white marble; notice the staircase by which the procession descended from the upper room, used for the rite of "refrigerio", to the inner burial room for the libation rite on the tombs of the deceased.

Mausoleum "E" – "Tomb of (T.) Aelius Tyrannus"
(Acorn and festoons above a cinerarium)

Mausoleum "E" – "Tomb of (T.) Aelius Tyrannus"
(Cinerarium with a Gorgon in relief)

MAUSOLEUM "F" – "Tomb of (M.) Caetennius Antigonus"

MAUSOLEUM "F" – "Tomb of (M.) Caetennius Antigonus"

This tomb was the first to be discovered. The top of the façade was uncovered when, in 1939, work was begun to lower the pavement of the Vatican Grottoes.

The names of members of the family are contained in many epigraphs, especially on the altar in the middle of the tomb. It is one of the largest and most ornate mausoleums.

On the façade, to the left of the entrance, there is a terracotta panel depicting a partridge; on the right-hand side there are architectural decorations.

The interior is rich with stucco figures and pictures of flowers and fruit; on the west wall there is a note-worthy rural scene. There are arcosolia and cineraria.

In this typically pagan tomb there is a burial that reveals some obviously Christian symbolism – a woman drawing water from a well, two doves with an olive branch, and the words *dormit in pace* – "rests in peace".

The deceased is a young Christian woman, Emilia Gorgonia; in the epitaph her husband recalls her beauty and goodness.

In another stone found in this tomb a wife eulogizes her husband, the director of a troupe of actors, and possessor of musical talent.

MAUSOLEUM "G" – "Tomb of the teacher"

MAUSOLEUM "G" – "Tomb of the teacher"

The fine structure of the façade of this tomb is in terracotta with graceful geometric designs. It is only possible to glimpse the remarkable delicacy of the ornamental frescoes of the vault and walls.

On the ceiling there are two gazelles depicted on the edges of a dark red rectangle, in the centre of which is a bird. On the far wall is a fresco representing two human figures, probably a teacher with his student.

MAUSOLEUM "H" – "Tomb of (C.) Valerius Herma"

MAUSOLEUM "H" – "Tomb of (C) Valerius Herma"

Before the tomb, on the eastern side of the façade is a sarcophagus of Parian marble depicting a hunting scene. It was probably used for Christian burial. The inscription includes such characteristic expressions as "BENEMERENTI", "DEPOSITIO". The sarcophagus is also decorated with two funerary genii holding the flaming torch of life, as well as palm branches and a peacock next to a basket.

On the south wall of the atrium there is a collection of stone tablets found in the tomb; some of them have ivy leaves as decoration.

One of these tablets is of notable interest; it is not classical, nor well-executed. The inscription is dedicated to "FLAVIUS ISTATILIUS OLIMPIUS", and on the upper right-hand corner it bears the solemn monogramme, "(☧)" unmistakably a Christian symbol. The epitaph describes the deceased as a very good man, jovial with all.

The western wall is a real columbarium, containing many cineraria.

This tomb is noteworthy because of its size, the largest of the Vatican Necropolis. The wealth of its ornaments and stucco decorations create one of the most interesting collections of art and treasures of pagan funerary rites.

The tomb contains typically pagan burials in cineraria or arcosoli; there are some Christian burials, evidenced by typical elements of primitive Christianity. All of the niches of the tomb are decorated with stucco figures of divinities and ancestors, characteristic of pagan cult. This tomb is characterized by its religious syncretism, its niches depicting figures of dancing satyrs and maenads.

The stucco and terra-cotta images of important family members clearly give evidence of the Egyptian funerary cult, which resounded in and penetrated the religious world and feelings of the Roman people.

Even the insides of the niches are decorated with figures, giving prominence to mythological figures; Oceanus, Tellus, Apollo, Isis, Diana, satyrs, and funerary genii can all be seen.

In the spaces of the vault above the niches there are garlands of fruit, flowers, funerary genii, and cornucopias filled with pomegranates and poppy flowers. Between the niches are some stucco Hermae with distinctly eastern hairstyles. Some terracotta sarcophagi are found in the tomb; they are not particularly decorated, and only a few of them contain acrostic inscriptions.

One beautifully-decorated sarcophagus has bas-relief busts of the couple buried there in the centre of the front; on the sides are sculptures of shields superimposed on spears.

Mausoleum "HH¹" – "Tomb of (C.) Valerius Herma"
(Detail of the North wall)

Mausoleum "H" – "Tomb of (C.) Valerius Herma"
(Detail showing "Oceanus" (above) and an ancestor)

Mausoleum "HH[1]" – "Tomb of (C.) Valerius Herma"
(Stone with the " ☧ " – Monogram of Christ)

Mausoleum "H" – "Tomb of (C.) Valerius Herma"
(Detail of a marble head of a man)

Mausoleum "H" – "Tomb of (C.) Valerius Herma"
(Detail of a marble head of a woman)

MAUSOLEUM "I" – "Tomb of the Chariot"

MAUSOLEUM "I" – "Tomb of the Chariot"

Tomb I, of the *Quadriga* – or Chariot – takes its name from the main figure of the mosaic pavement. White and black marble pieces depict the rape of Persephone by Pluto on a chariot driven by Mercury.

The border surrounding the mosaic depicts a series of animals, tigers and gazelles, among vases and flowering plants.

The frescoes present country scenes in which the viewer should notice a peacock, a duck, doves, and other birds, together with floral designs.

MAUSOLEUM "L" – "Tomb of the Caetenni"

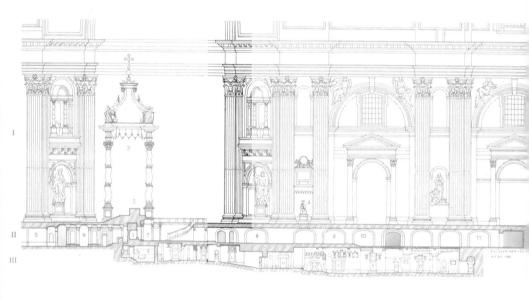

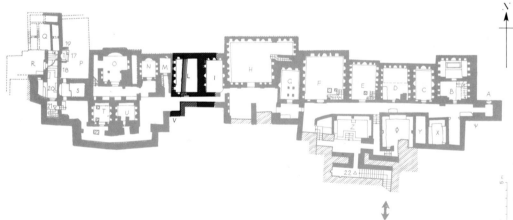

Detail of the cross section of the Basilica
and the map of the Necropols

MAUSOLEUM "L" – "Tomb of the Caetenni"

Although this tomb is mostly filled by a foundation wall, the "titulus" can still be seen; from it we learn the name of the owner.

Subsequent use of the tomb is forbidden by the formula HMHNS (Hoc Monumentum Heredem Non Sequetur*), which is included in the "titulus".

---

*This monument does not pass on to the heirs.

MAUSOLEUM "M" – "Tomb of Cristo-Sole"

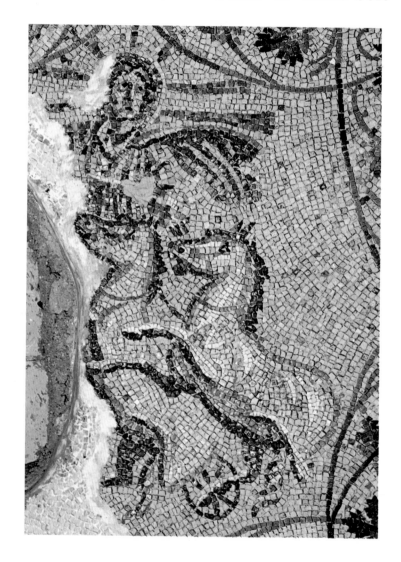

Ceiling mosaic of Cristo-Sole

MAUSOLEUM "M" – "Tomb of Cristo Sole"

The tomb of "Cristo Sole", that is Christ the Sun, was discovered in 1574, during some excavations beneath the Basilica.
According to Tiberio Alfarano, who meticulously copied the
epitaph which has since been lost, the tomb was built by the
parents of the deceased, Julius Tarpeianus.

The pagan origin of the tomb is obvious because of the presence of a cinerarium, although the three frescoes on the ceiling
and walls, which were decorated in polychrome mosaics, are un-
doubtedly Christian.

Christ is depicted on the vault in a chariot drawn by white
horses. The Good Shepherd was originally depicted on one of the
walls; the outline of a fisherman and a biblical scene including
Jonah appear on other walls.

Both vault and walls are decorated with grape vines.

Mausoleum "M" – "Tomb of Cristo-Sole" – North wall
(Lunette of the Fisherman)

Mausoleum "M" – "Tomb of Cristo-Sole" – East wall
(Lunette with the scene of Jonah)

MAUSOLEUM "N" – "Tomb of Aebutius"

MAUSOLEUM "N" – "Tomb of Aebutius"

The tomb of Aebutius also bears the name of "Clodius Romanus", who died at the age of twenty-one; his mother, Volusia Megiste, eulogizes him as her "most gentle son" on the epitaph of the cinerarium. This container offers some particulars of special significance, the Cup of sacrifice, the lighted lamp in the shape of a swan, and two vials for perfume.

In the same cinerarium, found among the human remains was a silver coin from the beginning of the second century A.D., probably from the time between Emperors Trajan and Hadrian. The presence of such a coin among the remains in an obviously re-used tomb bears witness to the existence of tombs in the Vatican already before the time of Emperor Trajan (98-117 A.D.), and also confirms that the Vatican Hill was a site used for burials.

Mausoleum "N" – "Tomb of Aebutius"
(Head of a young man surrounded by a laurel wreath
on the front of the cover of the cinerary urn of C. Clodius Romanus)

Mausoleum "N" – "Tomb of Aebutius"
(Cup and a swan-shaped lamp on the cinerarium
of C. Clodius Romanus)

THE AREA OF "FIELD P"

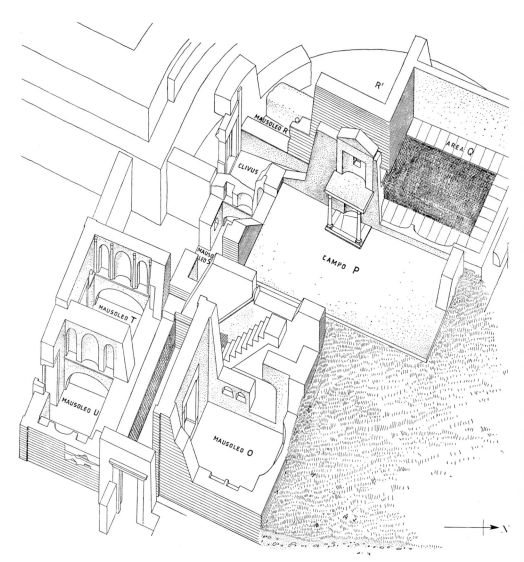

Axonometric projection of the central area and the mausoleums enclosing it.

MAUSOLEUM "O" – "Tomb of the Matucci"

In front of the ancient tomb of the Matucci is a small open enclosure with walls of opus reticulatum. To the west of the tomb is an external stairway which led to "Field P". The interior has cineraria in re-used niches.

The simple and austerely decorated walls are of plain yellow spaces, alternating with purple lines and delicate twigs with tiny leaves.

MAUSOLEUM "U"

The entrance to the tomb has been reduced because of a fault in the architrave. It is possible, however, to glimpse some of the niches with their characteristic red background and several arcosoli.

MAUSOLEUM "T" – "Tomb of Trebellena Flaccilla"

MAUSOLEUM "T" – "Tomb of Trebellena Flaccilla"

Tomb T contains evidence of some cineraria, as well as interments. There are some finely decorated niches with images of birds and flowers; the niches are separated by small stucco columns on a brightly-coloured background. There are some picturesque details, such as a dolphin wound round a trident and a vase between two doves.

In a cinerarium inscribed "Trebellenae Flaccilae Valeria Tæcina Matri dulcissimae fecit" was found a small bronze coin of the early Constantinian era with the inscription "Soli invicto comiti"; it can easily be traced to the Maxentian age.

MAUSOLEUM "S"

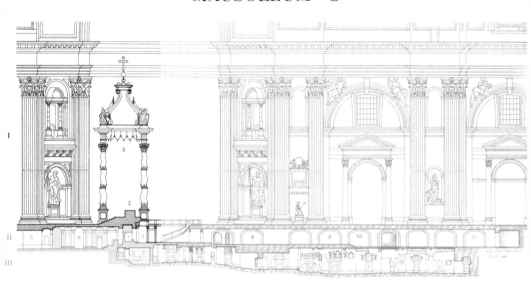

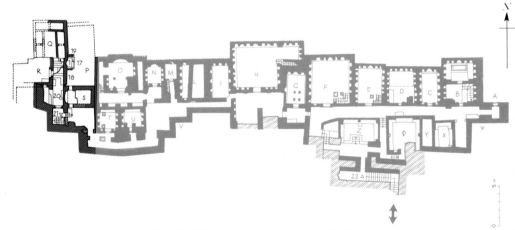

Detail of the cross section of the Basilica
and the map of the Necropols

MAUSOLEUM "S"

The foundations of the south-east column of Bernini's bronze canopy have been placed inside Tomb "S". Part of the façade with the threshold, and a small western section of the interior can be seen, including an arcosolium and some cineraria. This small tomb, however, is very important to help distinguish the famous "Field P", site of the burial of St. Peter.

Tomb "S" borders Field P to the south; Tomb "O" borders it to the east. Beyond the south-west corner of Tomb "S" is a small passageway, or "iter", proceeding from south to north; it is entered by way of a doorway.

This passageway, also known as the "Clivus" (20), is bordered on the right (east) by the western wall of Tomb "S" and the "Red Wall" (18); on the left, it is bounded by the front walls of tombs R and R[1].

The "Red Wall" is also a retaining wall, built to support the ground of Field P so that it would not sink or slide with the excavation that was needed to construct the Clivus leading to Tombs R and R[1], and Area Q to the north.

MAUSOLEUM "R" and "R¹"

MAUSOLEUM "R" and "R¹"

A large part of tombs R and R¹ is occupied by the foundation wall of the Bernini canopy and by sarcophagi placed there during the time of the Constantinian construction. A paleo-Christian sarcophagus flanked with the figures of Peter and Paul can be seen there.

From the entrance of the Clivus one can see a stairway which leads north towards Area Q; installed there in the Clivus is a drain which serves as a conduit for rain water. It is important from a chronological viewpoint; the tiles which cover it bear the stamp of the factories of M. Aurelius Caesar and Faustina Augusta. These stamps, therefore, help fix the age of the drain and the famous "Red wall", built at the same period as the "Clivus," shortly after the middle of the second century.

From the Clivus a series of steps proceed from south to north, reaching an area of tombs designated as "Area Q". In this area there are again tombs of interment, remains of a mosaic pavement of large black and white marble pieces, and several sarcophagi.

Mausoleum "R" and "R¹"
(The western face of the "Red wall"
as seen from the "Clivus")

AREA AROUND THE
TOMB OF ST. PETER

SOUTHERN AREA

Southern Portion of the "Memoria Costantiniana"

SOUTHERN AREA

You have now reached the level of Field P., that is the level of the "Trophy of Gaius".

The south column of this monument, enclosed within the Constantinian "Memoria", is still clearly visible. You can also see the south face of the altar of Callixtus II.

The Memoria of Constantine, which rose from the floor level of the apse of the basilica and was a part of that sacred area, has constantly been the centre and heart around which successive constructions were oriented.

Gregory-the-Great (590-604) built an altar for the celebration of the Eucharist above the tomb of the apostle. Thus, the presbytery of the Constantinian basilica was elevated and a semicircular crypt was built, which afforded the faithful an easier approach to the western side of the tomb of St. Peter, and, on the eastern side, delineated the sacred area of the "Confessio".

In building the "Confessio" and the semicircular crypt, Gregory clearly established two essential elements: the existence of the tomb, and the presence of the remains of the martyr Peter.

Callixtus II, in his turn (1119-1124) built an altar above that of Gregory, decorating it with valuable marble and cosmati.

WESTERN AREA

Clementine chapel

TO THE WEST

To the west one reaches the "semicircular crypt" which Pope Gregory had built to allow access to the tomb. From his area, now known as the Clementine Chapel because it was remodeled and decorated by Pope Clement VIII (1592-1605), it is possible to see the western wall of the "Memoria", the slab of purple veined marble and porphyry.

NORTHERN AREA

Northern area of the "Memoria Costantiniana"

Northern area of the "Memoria Costantiniana"
(The graffiti wall)

Northern area of the "Memoria Costantiniana"
(Detail of the graffiti wall)

Vatican Necropolis
(A votive offering and a brooch
found inside the "Memoria Costantiniana")

EASTERN ZONE

General view of the "Confessio Sancti Petri"

THE AREA OF "FIELD P"

The area known as Field P was the most venerated part of the cemetery; in fact, various tombs surrounded it, both respecting and honouring it, the tomb of St. Peter. A simple tomb, dug out of the ground, it is situated in the very centre of all the others because it was the tomb of the Apostle St. Peter, martyred during the persecution of Nero in the Neronian Gardens, between 64-67 A.D. This site has been the object of indisputable continuous veneration of the Church from the first century. Evidence has been confirmed by the discovery of walls and architectural materials which surrounded and rose above this sacred burial place.

A small monument was built directly over the tomb; a monument of niches — the Petrine funereal monument called the "Trophy of Gaius", spoken of by Gaius in the period of Pope Zephyrinus (199-217), between the end of the second and the beginning of the third centuries. This information was passed on to us by the historian, Eusebius of Caesarea. Throughout the centuries this monument was the nucleus; around it other structures were remodeled or added, never, however, obstructing the view of it.

The spot marked by the "Trophy" was found, during the excavations of 1940-1950, to be composed of a hole dug into the ground — this is the tomb of the apostle. Two niches were added, one above the other, beginning at ground level. Because of a serious fault on the northern section of the Red Wall, a small wall was built perpendicular to it; this wall is designated Wall "G" or the "Graffiti Wall", because of the various graffiti engraved in it.

Engravings, surnames, and funeral invocations to Christ are found here, written in the symbolic form of Chi-Rho, the celebrated Constantinian monogram. The site thus delineated, along with the architectural structures preserved and honoured through time, all take their name from the paleo-Christian Basilica, the "Apostolic Memorial of St. Peter".

From the East the "Memoria Apostolica" is now the "Niche of the Pallium".

The mosaic of Christ Pantocrator in the background of the niche rests on the east side of the Red Wall, roughly corresponding with the niches immediately above the tomb of St. Peter. In fact, the Niche of the Pallium has a small opening with a movable shutter, built to correspond with one found in the re-used slab of marble placed above the tomb when the "Trophy of Gaius" was built. This is the famous "Cataracta" by which the "Brandea" or small pieces of material for use as relics are lowered into the tomb.

According to the tradition of the Church, the Pallia have always been the symbols of true jurisdiction; they are given to the Pontiff and the Metropolitan Archbishops at the beginning of their ministry. Throughout the years, a time-honoured tradition has developed; the pallia are placed above the tomb of St. Peter; on the twenty-ninth of June, the Feast of SS. Peter and Paul, they are solemnly removed from the niche and placed by the Pope on the respective new Metropolitan-Archbishops.

From the tomb of Peter, that rock appointed by Christ to build his Church, the Pastors, under the guidance and example of the Vicar of Christ, Successor of Peter, are sent into the world to confirm their own brothers and the whole Christian people in the faith.

The "Niche of the Pallia" above the tomb of St. Peter

ACTA OF PIUS XII

RADIOMESSAGE

TO THE BISHOPS AND CHRISTIAN FAITHFUL OF THE ENTIRE WORLD

ON THE FEATS OF THE NATIVITY OF OUR LORD JESUS CHRIST, 1950.

REDISCOVERY OF THE TOMB OF THE PRINCE OF THE APOSTLES

If, during the Holy Year the "Confessio Sancti Petri" in the Vatican was the witness and centre of so many imposing demonstrations of the unity in faith and love of Catholics from throughout the world, the glory of this sacred place has been enhanced fulfilled in another sense as well: the excavations beneath that same "Confessio", at least as concerns the tomb of the Apostle and the scientific study which has taken place during this Jubilee Year (research which We have desired since the very first months of Our Pontificate) have been brought to a fortuitious end. In a very short time documented publication will make known the results of these thorough explorations.

These results are most rewarding and important. However, the essential questions are as follows: Has the tomb of St. Peter truly been located? To this question the conclusion of the work and study can clearly answer YES. The tomb of the Prince of the Apostles has beenfound.

A second question, subordinate to the first, concerns the relics of the saint. Have they been found? On the margins of the tomb some human remains have been found; however, it is not possible to prove with certainty that they belong to the mortal remains of the apostle. However, this has no effect on the historical truth of the tomb. The gigantic dome rises exactly above the tomb of the first Bishop of Rome, the first Pope; this originally simple tomb has had erected over it, due to the veneration of later centuries the greatest shrine in Christianity, a marvellous succession of works.

INDEX